Heavyweights

Contents

Written by Michele Paul

Rhinoceroses and Hippopotamuses

The World's Largest Land Animals

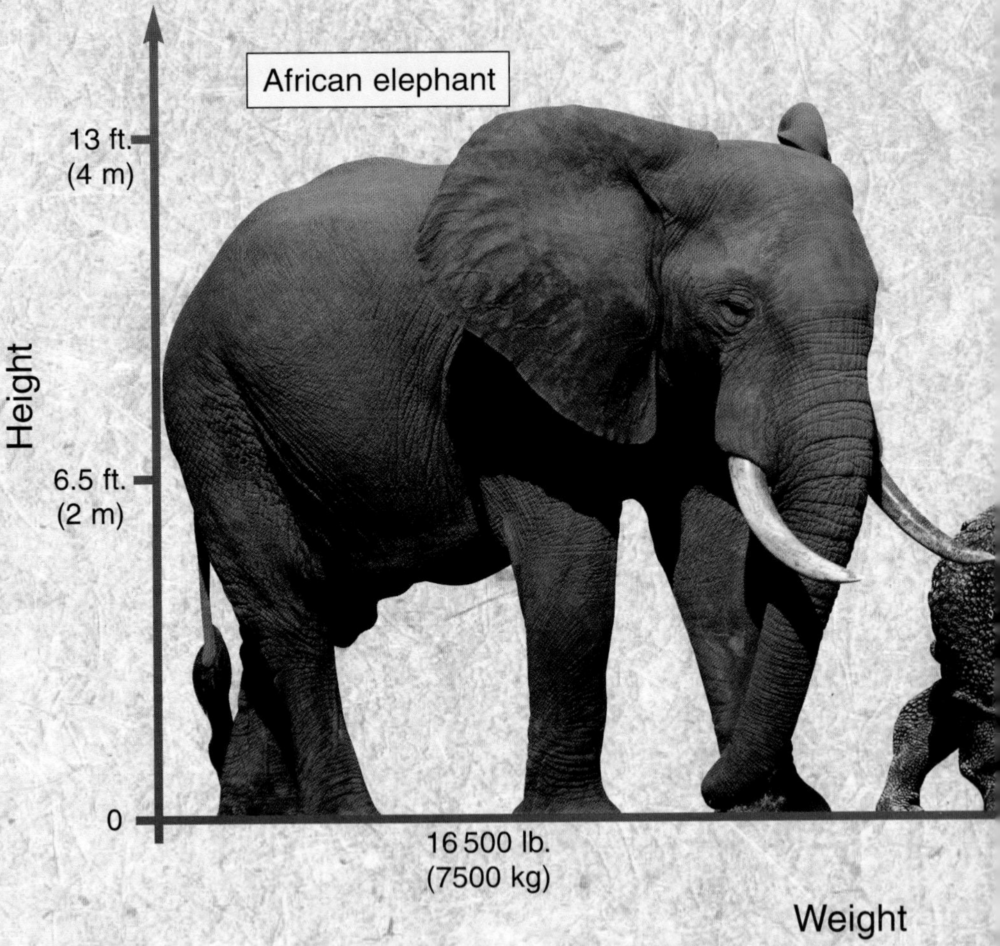

Animals come in all shapes and sizes. Some are big and some are small. The rhinoceros is the second biggest animal that lives on land, and the hippopotamus is the third biggest animal. The hippopotamus lives on the land and in the water. The biggest animal that lives on land is the elephant.

The name rhinoceros comes from a Greek word which means nose-horned. The name hippopotamus means river horse.

There are five types of rhinoceros in the world. They are:

- the black rhinoceros
- the white rhinoceros
- the Indian rhinoceros
- the Javan rhinoceros
- the Sumatran rhinoceros.

Rhinoceros and Hippopotamus Sizes

There are only two types of hippopotamus in the world. They are:

- the common hippopotamus
- the pygmy hippopotamus.

Even though the Indian Rhinoceros is taller than the common hippopotamus, the common hippopotamus weighs a lot more.

Places Where Hippopotamuses and Rhinoceroses Live

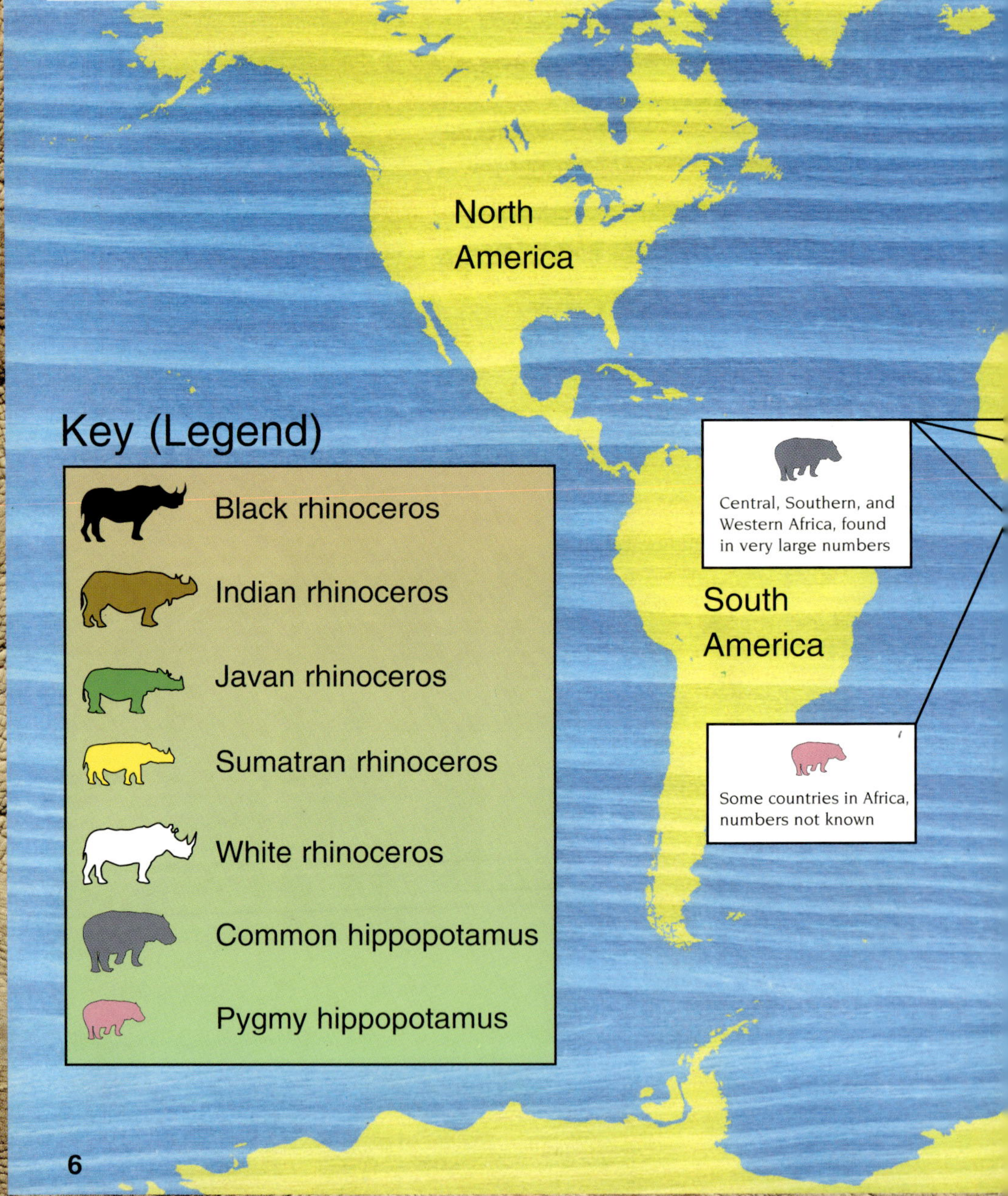

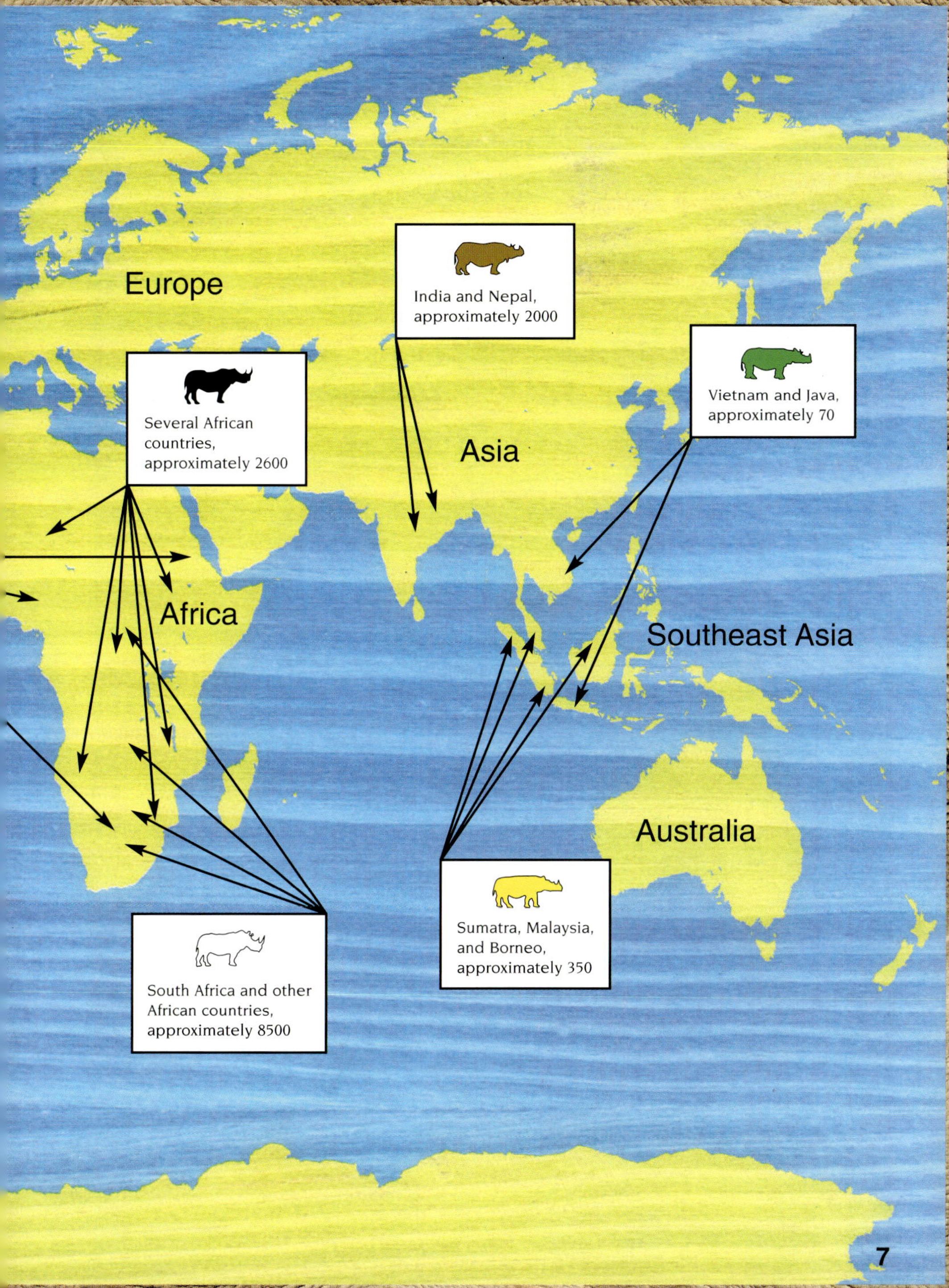
Europe
Asia
Africa
Southeast Asia
Australia
India and Nepal, approximately 2000
Vietnam and Java, approximately 70
Several African countries, approximately 2600
Sumatra, Malaysia, and Borneo, approximately 350
South Africa and other African countries, approximately 8500

Rhinoceroses

Rhinoceroses have solid bodies and short legs. They have one or two horns. Their horns are pointed and hard and are used for fighting or digging. Rhinoceros horns never stop growing and can grow up to 3 inches (8 cm) a year.

Rhinoceroses are very big animals but they can run very fast. Rhinoceroses have bad eyesight but very good hearing and they have a good sense of smell. Rhinoceroses' eyesight is so poor they sometimes charge at trees.

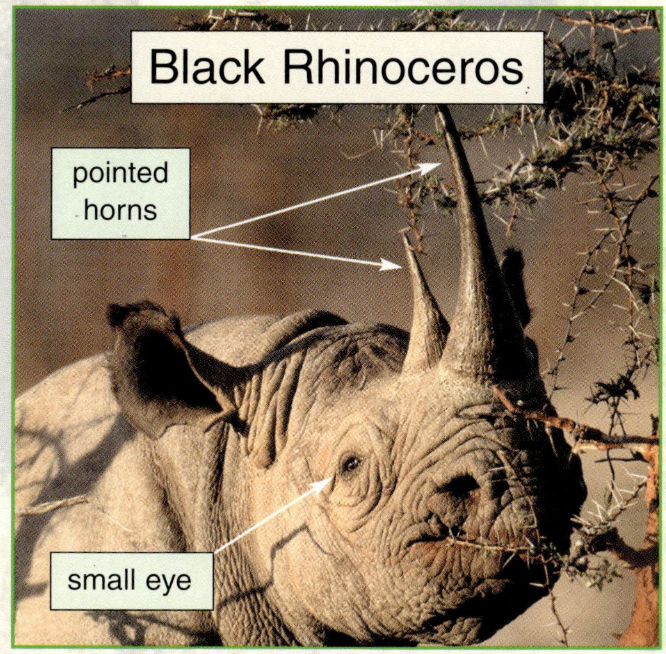

Indian Rhinoceros

What Does an Indian Rhinoceros Look Like?

The Indian rhinoceros is one of the largest rhinoceroses. The skin of the Indian rhinoceros hangs in folds. The Indian rhinoceros has only one horn. The horn can grow up to 24 inches (60 cm) long.

The legs of the Indian rhinoceros are very short. It usually walks but it can run at speeds of up to 35 miles (56 km) per hour.

The skin of the Indian rhinoceros hangs in folds.

How and Where Does an Indian Rhinoceros Live?

The Indian rhinoceros lives on grasslands and in forests where there are mud swamps. The Indian rhinoceros swims and wallows in mud. The mud coats its skin and protects it from getting burned by the sun. The Indian rhinoceros does not have any sweat glands so it uses mud to keep cool. The Indian rhinoceros uses a scent to mark out its territory.

The Indian rhinoceros feeds at night and in the early morning. It eats woody plants, grass, and shrubs. It drinks water every day.

The Indian rhinoceros eats grass, and birds eat insects that live on the rhinoceros.

Life Cycle of an Indian Rhinoceros

The female Indian rhinoceros carries her baby inside her for 16 months. An Indian rhinoceros calf weighs about 140 pounds (64 kg) when it is born. A rhinoceros calf is fed milk by its mother until it is one year old. A female Indian rhinoceros has a calf every three years. One week before she gives birth to a new calf, she chases away her last calf. In the wild, the Indian rhinoceros can live to about 40 years of age but in zoos it can live longer.

A mother rhinoceros and her calf hide in the grass.

Are Indian Rhinoceroses in Danger?

The Indian rhinoceros is killed for its horn, as some people think it can be used in medicines.

About 100 years ago the Indian rhinoceros was an endangered animal. There were only about 200 alive in the world. People have worked very hard to protect the Indian rhinoceros. Parks have been set up for them to live in and now there are about 2000 Indian rhinoceroses alive.

Indian rhinoceroses live in the Chitwan National Park.

Hippopotamuses

Hippopotamuses have large bodies, short legs, and very large mouths with ivory teeth. Hippopotamuses spend a lot of time in the water but they come on land to feed. When hippopotamuses come on land, they can walk and run very well.

Both the common hippopotamus and the pygmy hippopotamus have no hair on their bodies, apart from on their tails. They both make an oil to stop their skin from getting burned by the sun.

Common Hippopotamus

What Does a Common Hippopotamus Look Like?

The common hippopotamus has a very big head and its eyes stick out from its head. The ears, nose, and eyes of the common hippopotamus let it hear, breathe, and see when most of its head is under the water.

The common hippopotamus has a very large mouth. Some hippopotamus can open their mouths 4 feet (1.2 m) wide. Their teeth never stop growing and can grow to 2 feet (60 cm) long. The top and bottom teeth grind together, this stops them from growing too long.

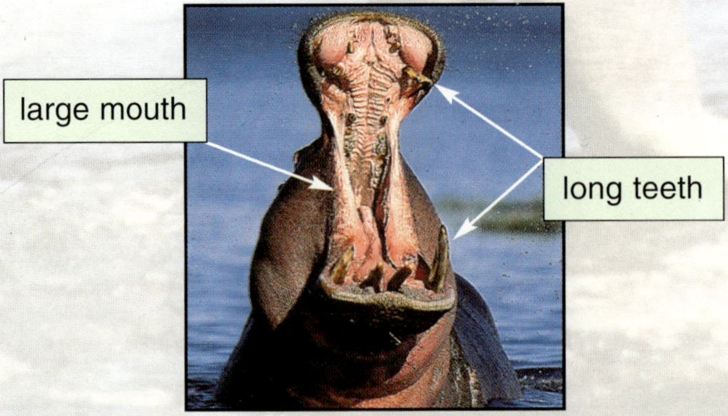

How and Where Does a Common Hippopotamus Live?

The common hippopotamus lives near grasslands in lakes, rivers, and streams. It lives with other hippopotamuses in herds of up to 30 animals.

The common hippopotamus spends the day in water, eating plants, and sunning itself in the sun. At night it comes on to land to feed. The common hippopotamus eats grass, fruit, leaves, and vegetables. It can graze for four or five hours each night and eat up to 88 pounds (40 kg) of food in one day.

Hippopotamuses rest on each other.

Life Cycle of a Common Hippopotamus

The female common hippopotamus carries her baby inside her for seven and a half months. The baby is born in water or on land. A hippopotamus calf weighs about 100 pounds (45 kg) when it is born. If a calf is born in water its mother helps it to swim. A calf is fed milk by its mother both on land and under the water. A hippopotamus calf starts to eat grass when it is about four months old. In the wild, hippopotamuses live to about 30 years of age but in zoos they live longer.

A hippopotamus calf eats grass when it is four months old.

Are Common Hippopotamuses in Danger?

The common hippopotamus is not an endangered animal. Humans are the biggest enemy of the common hippopotamus. Farmers have taken the lands where they graze. This means hippopotamuses are losing their homes.

Hippopotamuses are hunted and killed for their ivory teeth. The ivory of a hippopotamus is more valuable than the ivory of an elephant as it does not go yellow.

The ivory teeth of the common hippopotamus are very valuable.

Dangerous Heavyweights

Danger

Do not come near these animals.
You could get hurt.

Rhinoceroses and hippopotamuses are some of the largest animals on land, and they can hurt people and other animals. But rhinoceroses and hippopotamuses feed on grass or leaves, and they would only hurt another animal or person if they felt threatened.

Hippopotamus teeth can be very dangerous.

Danger to Heavyweights

Rhinoceros Numbers

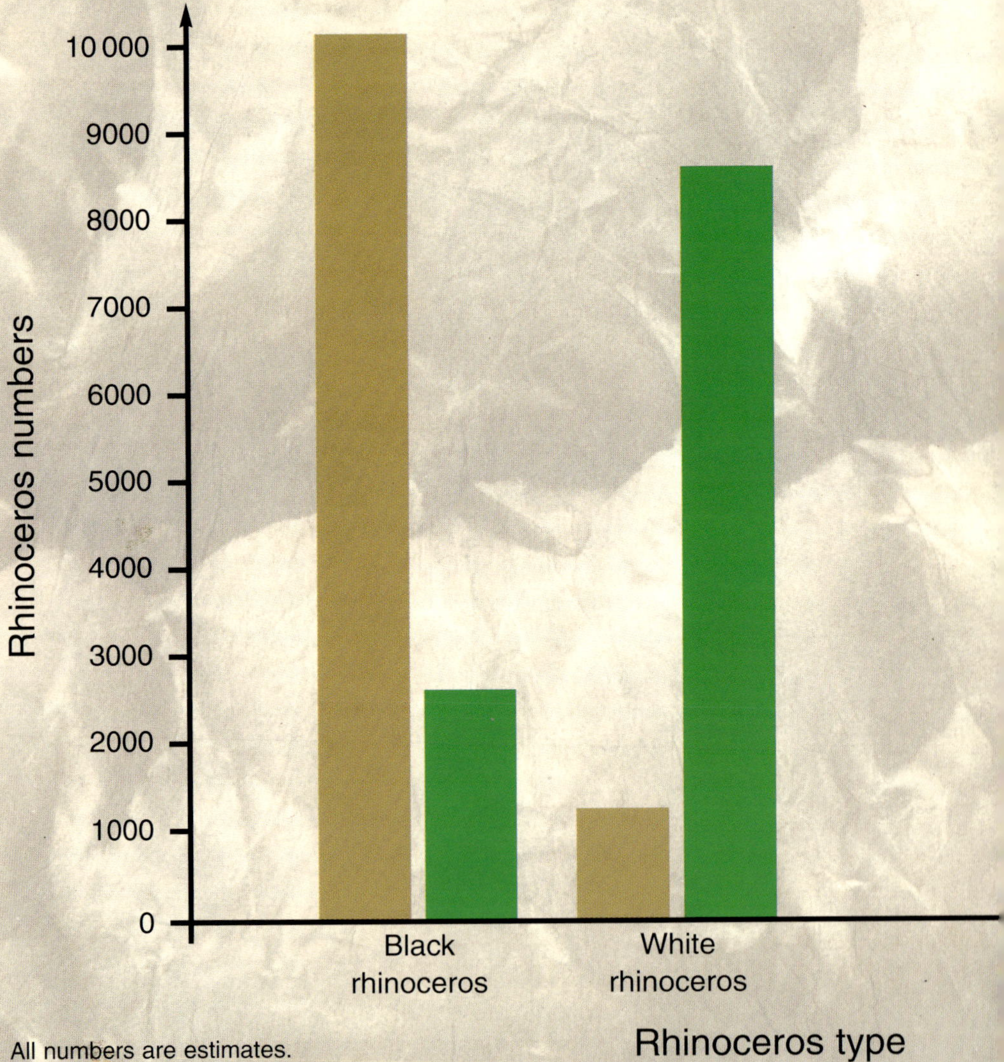

All numbers are estimates.

Both rhinoceroses and hippopotamuses have been hunted by humans and the lands they live on have been taken over by people. But it is the survival of the rhinoceros that is in danger.

All over the world there are people who do not want to lose rhinoceroses and hippopotamuses forever. They are working hard to make sure this does not happen.

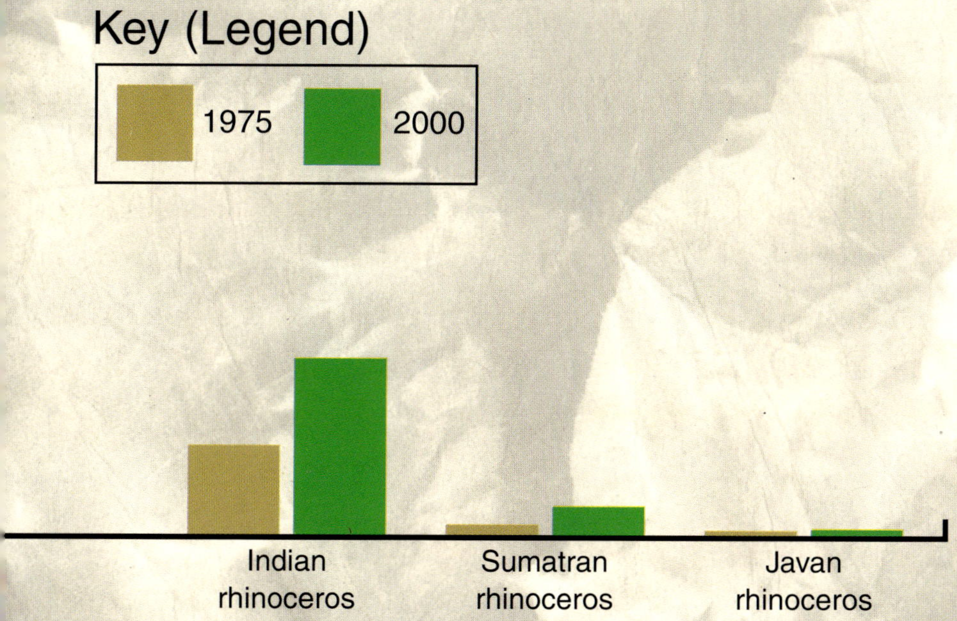

Glossary

When we do not know the exact number of something we are counting, we say **approximately**.

When there are not many animals left in a species, we say they are **endangered**.

Animals who **graze** eat grass and leaves.

Ivory is hard and white. Elephant tusks and hippopotamus teeth are made of ivory.

Something that is smaller than usual is sometimes called a **pygmy**, such as the pygmy hippopotamus.

For the **survival** of an animal species, there needs to be enough of the animals staying alive to have babies.

When animals are rolling around in mud or water, we say they are **wallowing**.